Wr ve to

le ad?

FOX EYE
PUBLISHING

Why do I have to learn to read?

Learning to read will help you to better understand the world around you.

Why will it help me to understand the world?

Because you will be able to read all the signs and labels you see ...

... and avoid making some horrible mistakes.

You will be able to learn
new skills, and do things
all by yourself.

Making things is much easier, once you have learnt to read instructions.

Reading stories can paint amazing pictures in your mind.

Amazing pictures
that are full of
fabulous creatures,
and wondrous places.

There is so much more you will discover once you have learnt to read.

# Let's find out about words and reading.

Turn the page over to discover the answers to these questions.

How big is the biggest book in the world?

What is the oldest printed book in the world?

What is the longest word in the English Language?

When was writing words invented?
How fast can people read?
How many words are there in the English Language?

Let's find out about words and reading.

The answers are ...

The biggest book in the world measures 5 m x 8.06 m (16.40 ft x 26.44 ft).

The Diamond Sutra, which dates back to 868 A.D.

It is: Pneumonoul-tramicroscopic-silicovolcano-coniosis (45 letters).

Cuneiform, an ancient writing system was in use over 5000 years ago.
On average, adults can read between 200 to 300 words per minute.
There are over 171,450 English words in current use.

# How to use this book

You can read this book with one child or a group of children.

The book can be used to begin a discussion around complex questions such as learning why we have to learn to read.

The book is also a reading aid, with enlarged and repeated words to help children to develop their reading skills.

# How to read the story

Before beginning the story, ensure that the children you are reading to are relaxed and focused.

Take time to look at the enlarged words and the illustrations, and discuss what this book might be about before reading the story.

New words can be tricky for young children to approach.

Sounding them out first, slowly and repeatedly, can help children to learn the words and become familiar with them.

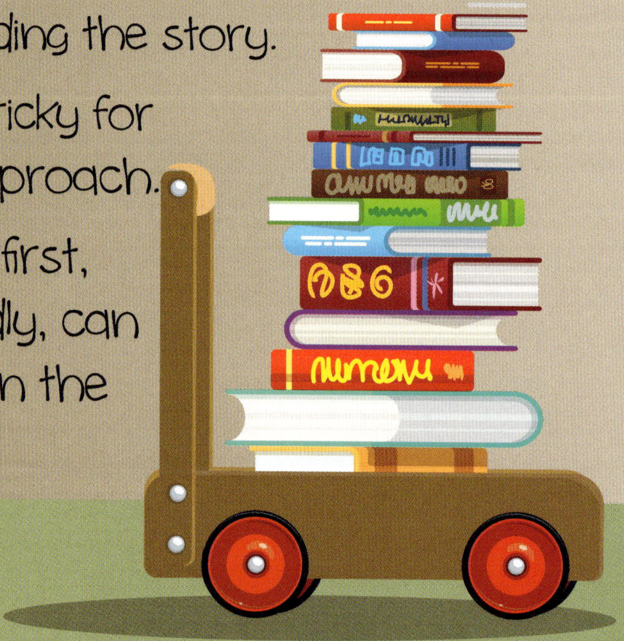

Did you spot
the Tardigrade
hiding in
this book?

First published in 2023 by Fox Eye Publishing
Unit 31, Vulcan House Business Centre,
Vulcan Road, Leicester, LE5 3EF
www.foxeyepublishing.com



Written and illustrated by Simon Couchman

ISBN 978-1-80445-354-4

A catalogue record for this book is available from the British Library.

Printed in China

# Titles in the Series

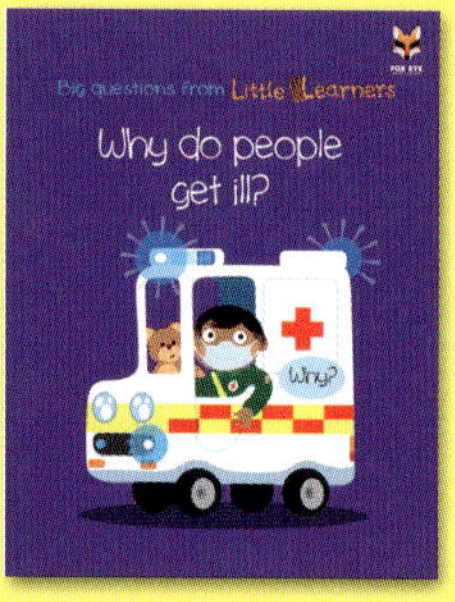


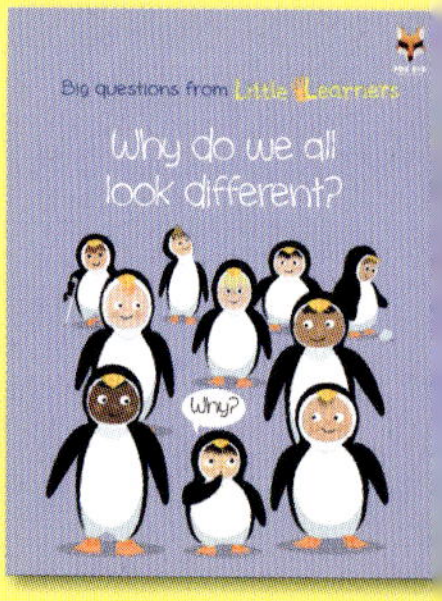

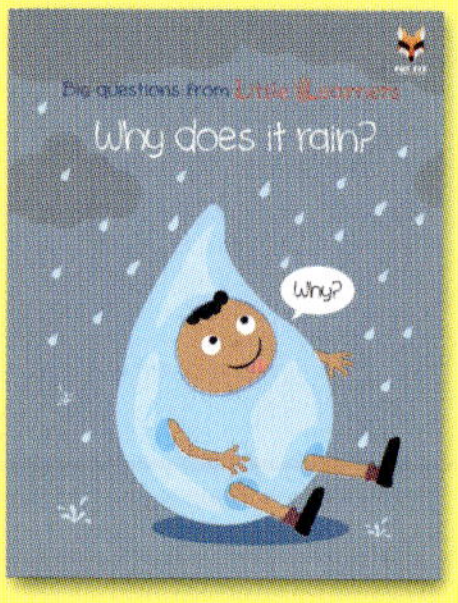